# ZEUS ALEXANDER PLUAS

# Collateral Damage

*The Anecdotes Of a Love Story That Born Life-Long Ramifications*

First edition

Editing by Jacqueline Flores Tomala

This book was professionally typeset on Reedsy.
Find out more at reedsy.com

# Contents

# DEDICATION

*To my wife Jacqueline, and our children, Zeus and Leilani, whom I genuinely care for, and to all those who picked up this book.*

*Thank you for taking a moment to hear from that child from long ago. Your feedback, questions, and shared experiences are treasures I truly value.*
*Feel free to reach out to me at zeusnjackie101@gmail.com*

# 2

# AMERICA! AMERICA!

Sometime in the mid-1960s, my father and grandfather were granted visas, and so they flew to New York City from Guayaquil, Ecuador. After a brief stint working in a factory, my father and grandfather opened up their own A/C and refrigeration repair shop in Brooklyn, New York. By that time, I, still a toddler, my older sister, mom and grandmother had joined them in America. One of my earliest childhood memories is sitting in my father's car, pretending to drive from the driver's seat, making engine sounds while turning the steering wheel left and right.

The apartment we lived in was quite shabby and desperately needed remodeling and a fresh coat of paint. We used to call that old apartment 'La Casa Vieja' which means The Old House. Christmas was great, though! After we had helped grandma with the Christmas decorations and with the adorning of the Christmas tree. Grandma would put on our favorite Christmas song which was called 'Mi Burrito Sabanero.' As grandma happily clapped and encouraged us, we would joyfully sing and dance around, all the while inhaling the obnoxious scent of melting plastic coming off of the lighted Christmas tree!

A few minutes before midnight, Grandma would rush us into the bathroom; and instruct us to brush our teeth, otherwise, Papa Noel wouldn't have any Christmas gifts for us. You see, back then, my parents didn't place our presents under the Christmas tree; instead, they put them under our beds just minutes before the clock struck midnight. Thus, traditionally, on the 24th of December, our elders had us stay up until twelve midnight, a request we very happily complied with so that we may receive our Christmas gifts. Which was unlike most American children who wait until Christmas morning to open their Christmas presents. Regardless, as soon as we were done brushing our teeth, we would run out of the bathroom to look straight under our beds and start pulling out one present after another!

I remember receiving the GI-Joe action figure with the wooly hair, beard, and scar. I always wondered how he got that scar in the first place, and tried to picture how that fight or battle went down. I also got an Electronic American Football game that emitted an annoying electric buzzing sound, even though I did not know how to play football nor did I comprehend it; all I knew was that you had to be big, tough, strong and fast.

Interestingly, my father probably knew even less than I did about Football. As a matter of fact, most Ecuadorians today do not know or could care less about American Football. So I imagine that in the early 1970s, American Football was not even on their radar. Regardless, I sometimes wonder what my parents must have been thinking or feeling as they stood there in the Lionel Playworld or a Toys-R-Us as they decided to buy me the Electronic Football game. For sure they must have felt that they were now a part of America. Even though neither one of my parents spoke any English. Nevertheless, they now have the means to proudly bestow upon me, their son, this outstanding piece of American technology! As a trophy by them, my parents, the

**new Americans! As, of course, America the Beautiful played on in their heads...**

*America! America! God shed his grace on thee*

*And crown thy good With brotherhood*

*From sea to shining sea!*

# 3

# Those Bitter Sweet OREOs

I do not remember what school I went to for kindergarten, but I clearly remember what should have been my first day in kindergarten. Even though the other kids were already in the classroom, apparently without a care in the world. I, on the other hand, was frightened, clinging to mom, and not wanting to ever let go.

I mean, I loved watching Romper Room, but I never said anything about wanting to leave the comfort and safety of home and be in it! Besides that, she is not Ms. Mary Ann, the nice and very pretty Romper Room lady whom I already had a crush on!

Anyhow, the teacher, after trying to persuade me to stay, suddenly makes an about-face, walks away, and disappears for a moment.She then leisurely starts walking back towards me with a beaming smile on her face, as if she had all the answers to help me overcome my fears.

Still with a beaming smile on her face, she bends down, and from behind her back, she pulls out a pack of OREOs and offers them to me. She indeed thought that she would be able to bribe me with some OREO cookies.

As anyone would have expected, that could have worked out well in most cases, but it turns out that I actually hated OREO cookies because, for me, they tasted bitter. Regardless, how dare she offer me such a thing!

Therefore, I smacked the pack of OREOs out of the teacher's hand, and she gasped in astonishment! Poor woman, she would have never guessed that I was the only kid in the world that hated OREO cookies, right? Now, anyone else would have been surprised at my lashing out, but mom should have seen it coming, because it was not the first time, nor the last, that I had ever displayed my dissatisfaction and reasserted my will ever so harshly.

One day, for whatever reason, maybe it was about OREOs, I was arguing with mom. So, to reassert my will and show my displeasure, I grabbed a leather Levi's belt with the brass-colored metal buckle and brought it down on my father's olive-green-colored organ/piano plastic thing!

My father didn't even know how to play the darn thing. But now, living in America, I guess that was his way of showing some class and sophistication a la Liberace, even though we lived in a shabby apartment where you had to reach overhead and pull on a rusty chain in order to flush the toilet!

Anyway, when my father arrived home from work, he found himself with a new and wonderfully toothless, olive-green-colored organ/piano plastic thing!

Thus, after I had smacked the pack of OREOs out of the teacher's hand. My mom roughly grabbed me by the arm, turned us around and we marched our way out of there!

On our way out, we see my older sister, Mildred, coming down a flight of stairs with the rest of her classmates. She looked just like Wednesday Adams rocking braids.

She saw us, waved at us with such a sweet smile, and said, ''Hi mommy, hi Zeus!'' My mother looked at me and said, ''See, your sister is a girl and she is not afraid!''

That was probably the first time I ever felt ashamed and was once again challenged. At that moment, I knew what Greg Brady must have felt like when he knocked the egg off of that traffic cone, thus losing his bet to Marcia. So I responded by saying, 'OK, I will stay.'' My Mother replied, ''It's too late; we will come back tomorrow!''

4

# PRESIDENT STREET

**B**y the time I made it to first grade, we had moved to an exceedingly nicer and much larger apartment on the third floor, located in a building on 1745 President Street in Crown Heights.

We had Lincoln Terrace Park just a few steps away from where we lived!

Most of our neighbors who lived in the surrounding homes were African American and Hasidic Jews. While most of the Hispanics lived in the apartment building, and were mostly Puerto Ricans. Even El Super was from Puerto Rico. He was a single dad raising four beautiful teenage daughters. I always wondered how he was able to handle all of that. There was this elderly white lady who lived in the apartment across the hall from us. Every so often she would squat right outside of the building's entrance and pee in public. The kids from the building started calling her 'La Vieja Sucia,' which means the dirty old lady. Sometimes, the kids would gather and play Ding-Dong with her doorbell. As soon as she started coming for the door, and angrily about to open it, we would run away screaming and laughing with exhilaration! She never ratted on us because we never overheard anything from El Super.

At any rate, we were the only Ecuadorian family in the building and the block, if not the entire neighborhood!

In the summer, now and then, the older Latino kids used to crack open La Pompa, or fire hydrant and everyone would jump around, and in and out of the gushing water.

There was always an older kid who would grab a can, most likely a can of Chef-Boy-Ar-Dee, or Habichuelas Goya opened on both ends, and place it in front of the fire hydrant to control the water like a jet stream.  It was a blast for us kids because that was our water park! However, the fun only lasted until the police or firemen came along to close the fire hydrant on us; fortunately, no one ever got in trouble with the authorities for having fun with La Pompa!

Every so often, we were lucky, and the free lunch truck would come along, handing out free lunches made up of peanut butter and jelly or Bologna sandwiches with either milk, apple juice, or orange juice. Water melons were also a big deal! Now and then, a box truck filled with watermelons would park on the street and start selling watermelons. My mother never failed to buy us a big ol' sweet watermelon. It was such a refreshing and delightful treat.

My sister Mildred and I were enrolled in a Catholic school named Saint Malachi. It had a Catholic church right on the premises. We even had our first communion there too. And my first grade teacher was Sister Nancy, she was very nice, and even dressed like a nun while we were in class. My two younger siblings, Johnny and Gina, stayed at home with mom.

My mother had become good friends with a Puerto Rican lady who lived on the second floor named Olga, who was very friendly and kind.

Olga had three sons: Richie, followed by Cano, and last, but not least, Lionel. We all became very close and were like family. Their apartment was on the second floor facing the street, so us boys used to camp out on their fire escape without any fear of falling down any stairs. We were just like brothers and we went everywhere together. Olga even became my little brother Johnny's godmother at his baptism, and she also enrolled Richie at the very same Catholic school we went to.

By the way, all the little kids in the neighborhood looked up to Richie; he was our leader. If some other bigger kid from another block came along, strutting his stuff and tried to bully or pick on us. we would go get Richie, who was always ready to fight for anyone on the block. Richie never lost a fight.

If the other kid knew who Richie was, they would back down. If they did not know Richie and decided to fight, they would get their butts kicked. Richie must have been like eleven years old, but he was still our hero! Later on, hearing that Richie had become a police officer with the NYPD, was no surprise at all.


So on school days, Richie, Mildred and I all used to catch a public bus right down the street in front of the park on Rochester Ave. Sometimes my mother would wait with us at the bus stop.

So there we were, just three grade school kids, wearing Catholic school uniforms with our book bags and metal lunch boxes, on our way to school on a public bus.

The best part of the school day for me was cracking open my Evel Knieval metal lunch box and grabbing that delicious, albeit super soggy, tuna sandwich that mom prepared for me everyday!

Oh man, the scent lingering in the lunch box after I was done eating was pure ecstasy!

# 5

# OUR DISNEYLAND

Around that time, my father and grandfather had moved their AC and refrigeration repair shop to Avenue A, between East 9th Street and St. Mark's Place, and right across the street from Tompkins Square Park in Manhattan.

My father drove every morning from Brooklyn to the shop to work and do house calls. On some Saturday mornings, we used to all jump in the car to go see our grandparents, who were now living in Manhattan, and hang out at the shop.

There were some people coming through on Avenue A or hanging around the park that we called winos. We more than likely picked up that term from watching cartoons. Anyway, those people were suffering from some kind of addiction, while others freely walked around with obvious mental health issues.

I remember there was this one old man that reminded me of Wimpy from Popeye. He always wore a long, thick wool coat, even in the summertime!

I used to believe that that coat was like a shell for him. So I used to imagine that he would lie down anywhere, pull in his legs, arms, and head, and go to sleep inside of his coat like a turtle. Other times I would imagine that he had the ability to easily spread his coat open, trap a kid inside, and then quietly walk away without anyone noticing. Therefore, whenever I saw him coming down the block, I would run back into the shop and hide behind a fridge until the coast was cleared.

There was another young blond white dude. He must have been in his 30s, had a full beard, and always wore a dark blue-colored, short sleeve button shirt, matching pants, and work boots. He looked just like a car mechanic. Every time he walked down Avenue A. He never failed to pop into our repair shop and start speaking to us in gibberish. He was a big guy, tall, solidly built, and with massive hairy forearms.

Sometimes my father was out doing a house call, or delivering a fridge with the hired help. Hence, every so often, we would be at the shop waiting with grandma and grandpa whenever the big guy would pop in all of a sudden! He would stand in front of the shop's entrance. Making us feel trapped off! He would then stare into our faces with a far-off look in his blue eyes and begin speaking gibberish. It was terrifying for us, so we would all huddle around our grandparents. Neither one of them spoke or understood much English, so they had no idea what his gibberish was about, and neither did we.

Nevertheless, my grandparents remained very calm, merely stared back at him and slightly nodded their heads. I used to look at my elderly grandparents, and in my mind say to myself, 'Man, if he goes off or comes down with some kind of manic episode, we are fudge!'

Well, after what felt like an eternity, which was probably just a minute, he would simply do an about-face and leave. Sometimes he would be licking an Ice-cream cone, but we never got used to that because it was always scary!

At any rate, there was a Pizzeria right on the corner; I believe the slice was 35 cents. Right next door to us, there was a Greek coffee shop whose owner sometimes came over with free donuts for us kids to munch on.

We would always watch in amazement as the Hells Angels frequently came thundering down Avenue A on their choppers. That was a sight to behold! Every so often, people would gather in Tompkins Square Park to see musicians and bands play. It was all very exciting for us kids because this part of Avenue A was like our Disneyland!

# 6

# FROM AMERICA WITH LOVE

We started visiting a travel agency called Delgado Travel. Visiting that travel agency had become like a holiday for us.

I thoroughly enjoyed looking at the model airplanes that were displayed. That environment made me feel as if the promise of a wish was about to come true, even though my father was there for business.

He had started investing in all kinds of American, Made in the USA merchandise. He would invest in all kinds of stuff from shoes/sneakers, clothing, cologne/perfumes, TVs, and radios etc.

My father would ship all that merchandise in wooden crates, which he made himself out of plywood. He even shipped himself a couple of cars: a Ford LTD and a Gran Torino station wagon.

Back then, American -made goods were in high demand, and people in Ecuador admired both American-made products and cars with automatic transmissions.

As follows, he started traveling back to Ecuador, and soon he began making frequent trips,and each time he would stay away from us for more extended periods.

After he returned from a trip to Ecuador, we knew that he was merely going to stay for a few weeks in New York.

Whenever he was gone, we felt somewhat uncertain because we never fully understood why he had to stay away for so long while conducting business in Ecuador. Regardless, whenever he was away, it did not keep us from asking Mom when Papi was coming home over and over again. That was our version of, 'Are we there yet?' My mother never responded, though. She would merely stare at us with a blank look on her face and not say anything.

Then one day, after my father had returned from one of his trips to Ecuador, we packed up and moved to a 1st-floor apartment on 5745 Granger Street in Queens.

On moving day I was very sad moving away from Olga and her sons. It was the very 1st time I ever felt such great disappointment. Nevertheless, we got used to Queens very quickly.

Although Flushing Meadow park was a bit of a distance compared to Lincoln Terrace park, which was right down the street from where we lived before, at least the new apartment had a yard and a swing set that my parents had recently purchased for us.

Anyhow, since we had moved to Queens, we were no longer enrolled in a Catholic school. I am not sure if it was because we couldn't afford it, given that my father was away most of the time making money while doing business in Ecuador.

Instead, we started attending P.S. 14 Queens, which, nonetheless, was a nice school with excellent and very caring teachers. In any case, we no longer had to catch a public bus to get to school; instead, we walked since it was just a few short blocks away.

In Queens the neighborhood was quieter and looked even prettier after it had snowed. By then, my father was never again home for the holidays. For the last few years, it has been just Mom and us adorning the Christmas tree. As far as gift wrapping, my mother used to take care of that by herself, late at night after we had gone to bed.

I remember struggling to stay awake to hear the gift wrapping, as if I would be able to tell what I was getting for Christmas just by listening, but all I was able to make out was my mother sobbing while she was wrapping our presents. Regardless, Mom always made sure we had a nice and joyous Christmas.

This time around for Christmas, I got Elektroman, The Fonz, Pulsar, another Bionic Man, just to name a few. My older sister got a Barbie styling head, Tiffany Taylor, Sonny and Cher, Donny and Marie amongst other things.

I am not able to remember what my younger siblings received since they were much younger, but I sure remember all of the great toys that I had received, though.

I remember the last Christmas we had collectively with my father was back in Brooklyn on President Street. Back then, we received toys like the Lone Ranger, Rock Em Sock Em Robots, Evel Knievel Stunt Chopper, The Bionic Man with his Bionic eye that made things look farther away than up close like in the series, and the absolutely amazing Marx Best Of The West collection. I remember my sister Mildred got a Baby That Away, among other things!

After we had been living in Queens for about two years, my mother, a few times per week, was on the telephone speaking with some mystery woman. It turns out that our father, who was now around 34 years old, had met a younger woman, and had started a love affair with her.

Each time Mom was on the phone speaking to some mysterious

woman, we would pay attention. It is rumored that the caller was, in fact, the sister of the other woman. Allegedly, she was reporting all of my father's activities while he was in Ecuador. The speculation is that she was unhappy about her younger sister dating an older married man with children.

Many times, as we watched TV and the Spiderman theme song joyfully played in the background, my heart was simultaneously filled with fear and doubt.

While trying to sing along to the Spiderman theme song, I couldn't help overhearing what my mother was acknowledging over the phone...

*Spiderman, Spiderman,*

*Does whatever a spider can...*

''So he is seeing another woman!''

*Spins a web of any size...*

''They say she is younger!''

*Catches thieves just like flies...*

''He is going to build her a house!''

*Look out!...*

''Says he is going to ask me for a divorce!'

*Here comes the Spiderman!*

''I will never give him a divorce!''

It was no longer a secret. My mother never said anything, but we had heard enough to discern what had been going on with my father, and we even knew the name of my father's girlfriend. It was Monica! Whenever we heard that name mentioned, it was as if they were summoning up a demon from hell!

# 7

# THIRD WORLD DICTATION

By the summer of 1979, we were already on welfare. We never got used to the landlord knocking on our door, trying to collect the rent money that we no longer paid on time. Sometimes we answered the door, and other times we acted like we were not home.

As it turned out, my mother had decided to go after my father. Instead of paying the rent, she was saving it and selling our stuff so that we could all travel to Ecuador.

In other words, after the cat had been out of the bag, my mother uprooted us to chase after my father, even though their relationship had pretty much been over since 1975 or so. For the last few years, my father had proved that he cared more for his sweetheart than he did for my mother and his children. Even today, I still wonder why Mom decided to go after a man who did not care about us.

While she was alive, I never thought of asking her about that just to avoid bringing up so many bad memories.

I understand why my father abandoned us, but even now, I find it difficult to accept why Mom would place her children in such a predicament.

One day, I asked my aunt why Mom had made such a terrible decision in chasing after Dad, and my aunt responded by saying that my mom was trying to save her marriage because she still loved my father. Therefore, according to popular belief, Mom did it out of love?—how ironic!

As a result, in the summer of 1979, we took a flight out of JFK on Braniff International.

When we arrived in Ecuador, we stayed at my father's old family home, where my aunt still lived. My siblings and I were shocked, disappointed, and in awe of how shitty and creepy everything was in Guayaquil, Ecuador, including that house!

In New York, we were not a wealthy family, but we went from having a working stove, a fridge and a pantry always filled with food to having no fridge, stove, or food conveniently there for us at all times!

We went from a pleasant apartment to living in an old house infested with mice, rats, roaches, spiders, centipedes, and occasionally scorpions! The mosquitoes at night were also a problem.

The floors on that house were bare termite infested wooden planks. It had a very hot tin roof with no ceiling nor insulation. Termite pellets used to rain down on everything every single day. The walls were made out of dusty red brick and bare.

Then, living in Guayaquil, earthquakes were a new and terrifying experience for us. During quakes, that house would rock and sway like a boat on rough seas. Caught off guard, our legs would feel like jello, rendering us immobilized right on the spot, not knowing what to do or where to run and hide.

The earthquake on August 18th, 1980, was particularly severe. Nevertheless, every time the ground shook, it was quite frightening.

Power outages were also a common occurrence, happening many times per month, mostly in the evenings. People would pull out old rubber car tires and set them on fire in the middle of the street. The entire neighborhood smelled of burning tar, and the fumes were more obnoxious than the smell of burning plastic emanating from our old Christmas tree of yesteryear. Before this, the only black out I had experienced was in the summer of 1977. The word on the street was that a meteor had crashed in New York City.

Anyway, in Guayaquil, water supply was limited to a couple of hours a day, and the pressure was almost a trickle. We had to collect water in buckets for bathing and flushing the toilet. Speaking of toilets, unfortunately, even toilet paper became a luxury. So, many times, we resorted to the traditional Ecuadorian practice of using pieces of newspaper to wipe our butts after doing #2. Ouch!

We went from watching awesome cartoons everyday, especially on Saturday mornings, to having to wait until noon for the TV stations to begin their broadcast in Ecuador. No more Super-Friends for us, or the rest of the cartoons that we knew and enjoyed so much; now there were a whole lot of Japanese cartoons that we had never seen or even heard about.

The closest thing to a Japanese cartoon that we ever watched while in New York was 'Battle Of The Planets.' Well, some Japanese cartoons, like Mazinger, were cool, and at least we were able to watch Looney Tunes in Spanish.


No more American Bandstand, Soul Train or WABC-AM radio! Now we have to keep up with the latest American music hits by watching a show on Saturdays also called Soul Train, but without the dancers!

Its Afro- Ecuadorian host had an uncanny resemblance to Don Cornelius, and he even sounded like the Don!

No more Happy Days, literally, or Three's Company, Brady Bunch reruns; now there are reruns of Bonanza and some series called Combat, in black and white too.

No more Let's Make a Deal, Family Feud, or The Price Is Right, etc.

I mean, when Farrah Fawcett left Charlie's Angels, I was devastated. Whenever I listened to the song 'Heaven Must be Missing an Angel,' you couldn't argue with me that they were not singing about Farrah because, in my heavenly thoughts, she was my missing angel!

But what we were facing then and there in Ecuador was off the charts ridiculous!

No more cereals that were 'part of this complete breakfast!' along with an egg omelet topped with a KRAFT single, some bacon or breakfast sausages, and hot cocoa.

Now, it was one piece of bread, freshly baked, and butter, with a cup of black coffee. Black coffee for us kids in a country that is known for its cocoa.

In Ecuador they called breakfast 'coffee,' and that was exactly what they served us for breakfast!

Then my mother enrolled us in school, and that experience was just as challenging because I could hardly comprehend anything they taught or said!

There were no textbooks at all; instead the teacher dictated every-thing mercilessly. In my mind, I kept asking myself, 'Hold up! What are 5th graders doing taking down dictation? Isn't that for grown-ups, secretaries, and big people!'

Anyhow, while the dictator dictated, I was squirming in my seat and fumbling, trying to keep up. He might as well have grown a toothbrush mustache and marched me into battle!

I was miserable. Holidays like the Fourth of July, Halloween and Thanksgiving were non existing. Worse of all, no more of that American Christmas spirit that we enjoyed so much, or a white Christmas, or any Christmas at all.

The best we got was a live turkey that my aunt bought for Christmas. So we got to see it get butchered after my aunt had twisted its neck. The poor thing had run around the kitchen with its head flopping all over the place, before it even dropped dead!

After witnessing that, and for the rest of his life, my little brother Johnny refused to eat any poultry dish that was served, unless it was Kentucky Fried Chicken, of course!

8

# THE BARREN WASTELAND

While in Ecuador, my aunt had pointed out the other woman to my mother. Ironically, back in New York, we had heard the rumors about my father being with Monica during family gatherings. My aunt, who got along well with Monica, and the rest of my father's family had given their blessings to my father and Monica.

This always weighed on me. I used to ask myself, why would my family support that relationship—a relationship that had caused my father to neglect his children, did we not matter at all?

As soon as my mother knew who Monica was, Mom began stalking her. As a matter of fact, Monica was still in her teens and in high school! Now and then, Mom would sit outside that high school, waiting to intercept Monica on her way out.

Mom would try to convince that young lady to stop dating my father. I am certain it must have been like trying to persuade a stubborn child to do something they did not feel like doing. Anyhow, Mom was never able to gain any ground, and things were about to get worse.

One day, my mother decided to speak with the other woman's mother and hauled us along. My mother had planned to introduce us to Monica's mom. In doing so, she would see who the children of her daughter's lover were. With the hopes that, after she met us, it might compel or obligate her to encourage Monica to end her relationship with that married man who fathered those poor little ones.

No doubt, Mom believed she could appeal to Monica's mother's sense of morality for the sake of our well-being, ironically. However, considering how poor Monica and her family were, my father was indeed providing essential resources. Given this, Monica and her mother were unlikely to forfeit the benefits they received from my father just for our sake.

Regardless, on that day, we all hopped in a taxi, and off we went to confront Monica's mother. I believe we were heading south, it felt like we were leaving the city behind as the asphalt disappeared, and we found ourselves on a dirt road in a flat, barren wasteland. I don't recall whether we were heading towards an area of Guayaquil called El Guasmo or El Suburbio, but it was indeed one of the two.

I do know that El Guasmo, in the 1970s, consisted of flood plains unsuitable for urbanization and lacked basic services. I believe El Suburbio was just as challenging a place. Nevertheless, the poorest among the poor invaded the area. The landscape remains vivid in my memory, consisting of dirt and mud with houses sporadically scattered, made of cane and elevated on stilts.

After traveling a considerable distance, the cab made a left turn, and suddenly, like magic, my father's Ford LTD. came to a stop in front of us. I'm not sure if we had followed him, or perhaps we had been following him for some time, but I had not noticed due to my distraction and awe of the surrounding landscape. Nevertheless, I also noticed that my father had a passenger: it was the other woman!

Turns out, this is the very first time we all saw our father together with the other woman. Therefore, I do not doubt that Mom must have seen red!

Hence, in what seems to have been a split second, next thing you know, she is jumping out of the cab and is off running towards the LTD, and she reaches it in no time and is now opening the passenger side door. The gloves were off; it was war! My mother had delivered us into the trenches, even though we were vulnerable and fighting a war that we did not quite fully understand and that had already been lost long ago.

So, with great force, she reaches within with one arm and pulls Monica out of the car by her hair, drags her through the ground, and proceeds to beat the hell out of her! By the time my father got out of the driver's side and came around to pull Mom off of Monica, we kids were already out of the cab, huddled together, frightened to death and crying. Watching this terrible scene play out before me, filled me with a sense of dread, and at that moment, I had never felt so vulnerable and isolated. My father was ultimately able to get my mother off of Monica, and he forced my mother into the passenger seat.

He then picked Monica up by her arm, and she looked like a stubborn child. A stubborn teenager whose father had come to get her after she had refused to come inside after hanging out with her friends. He delivered her over to her mother, who had come outside looking in disbelief. He then had us get in the rear seat. As my father pulled away, I felt numb, and my siblings sobbing sounded like a haunting melody of impending doom.

My mother kept cursing and saying things that I no longer recall. All I remember is the fury in her eyes while she spewed her verbal assault on my father, who was calm and just kept asking her to shut up.

Nevertheless, during her verbal assault, Mom must have said something that was true. Because this caused my father to fling his right arm towards my mother's face! It sounded like a whip striking a pool of water.

Mom gasped! I looked at her and watched as she lowered her head slowly and began to quietly sob and whimper. I can only imagine all of the hurt and regrets she must have been feeling then. The scene was distressing, and I bore immeasurable sorrow, but at the same time, it filled me up with so much rage and valor.

At that moment, all I desired was justice, to undo the harm that I had just witnessed, and to break free from all of the disillusionment.

So I screamed in Spanish, 'NO LE PEGUES A MI MAMIII!' As if screaming, 'Don't hit my mommyyy!' and drawing out, or extending the very last syllable would have been able to tare down walls and disintegrate everything that I had been harboring. Immediately after this, I instinctively jumped on my father from behind and started hammering down punches to the back of his neck, head, and shoulders!

As he drove, he kept one hand on the steering wheel, and all he could do to attempt and keep me off of him was to awkwardly try and push me off with his right arm. He ultimately stopped the car, turned around, and was now throwing awkward punches with his left arm toward my midsection as I kept fighting back, now kicking up with both my legs to try and match his reach! With each jab, he kept repeating, 'YA YA YA,' as if I was an animal to be tamed. But I did not want to stop, and I merely did after my mother pleaded with me.

# 9

# I LOVE NEW YORK

On the drive back, I felt trapped in an endless pit. At that moment, I could have described what the thousand-yard stare was because I knew what it felt like. I believed that nothing worthy existed anymore. The realization that I had no home, no father, no country, no peace of mind, no school and no future along with a broken family was all too real.

Traveling on that dirt road through that deserted and barren wasteland, I saw my previous life and memories from Brooklyn, Queens, Manhattan,... My friends, my school, my toys, and what had been my home on President and Granger Street were all now just a far-off dream. As if they had never existed and were all about nothing, or to have traded all of that for this!

So that I may be an 11-year-old boy already wishing to return to the past as I traveled on that dusty road through a barren wasteland.

Trapped in a moving vehicle with a man who was presently a foe and an enemy while I had no way out. My mind played the, 'I Love New York' song wishing that it would magically take me away and back to the previous life I had known and missed so much.

After that debacle, my mother returned to New York to work for a few months. Upon her return, she had saved enough money for our journey back to the U.S.A. I was delighted because I thought that by returning to New York City, we would be able to continue our lives where we had left off.

But it turns out that my mother had decided to have us live in Miami, Florida, away from the rest of my father's family. I was content to be leaving Ecuador, but I felt disappointed that we were heading to Miami instead of New York.

I was afraid of facing a new reality and believed that I would never be able to adjust to another new environment.

Upon arriving in Miami, we were malnourished, infested with parasites, depressed and afraid. We had nothing, except for the clothes we were wearing.

My mother had an Ecuadorian friend who lived in Miami Beach. So we stayed at her friend's place until we were able to get on welfare and in an apartment on 15th Street in South Beach.

We were now surrounded by a non-stop parade of retired senior citizens and Cuban refugees from the Mariel boat lift.

I, too, felt and looked like a refugee in a new land with nothing but the clothes off my back.

We arrived in time for Mom to enroll me in summer school at Nautilus Junior High, and, once again, I was afraid, wishing desperately not to go. But this time around, I couldn't cling to Mom, and there wasn't a teacher offering a pack of OREOs, which, now, I would have gladly accepted to soothe my fears.

Because of the drug trade issues in Miami during the early 1980s, my mother was under the impression that drugs were also being freely distributed in school.

So,on my first day, she advised me not to accept drugs from anyone. However, I certainly didn't need any drugs, as I was already emotionally and physically messed up. What I probably needed was counseling or therapy, which I never received, and no one realized that I was a kid in need of such help.

In 1981, at Nautilus Junior High, all the cool kids were wearing corduroy Levi's and/or designer jeans like Jordache, Sergio Valente, and Izod Lacoste/Polo shirts, and Nike track suits. As far as footwear went, they were rocking Nikes and/or leather boat shoes.

When we were growing up in 1970s New York City, Pro-Keds, and Chinese slippers were what we rocked. By the way, in New York City, most kids felt that they would be able to do Kung-Fu and beat somebody up just by wearing those Chinese slippers.

We felt especially inspired when the song 'Kung Fu Fighting' came out. Having seen countless Kung Fu movies on 42nd Street, we thought we already knew some Kung Fu. Anyhow, soon after that it was Pumas and Wallabees.

However, now living on South Beach, we could not afford the name brand of anything. My shoes, for instance, were some imitation boat shoes that my mom picked up for me for $2.99 from the local Pantry Pride.

My mother's Ecuadorian friend had a son who used to look at me, sing, 'BoBos cost a dollar ninety-nine. BoBos make ya momma feel fine,' and then he would burst out laughing! I felt like jumping out of my skin or punching him in the face, but he was stronger, more athletic, and heavier than me.

On the other hand, I was weak, scrawny, and afraid. I couldn't even run a lap in Mr. Friedman's P.E. class at Nautilus without almost passing out and vomiting!

So instead, I would fake a laugh to try and show bravery, but deep inside, I felt profoundly humiliated and dehumanized whenever he sang that BoBos song to me. This was especially true knowing that, out of pity, his mother forced him to hang out with me, however infrequently it had been.

# 10

# LUNCH TIME AT NAUTILUS

I felt like an outsider while attending Nautilus Junior High in the 7th grade. Lunchtime was particularly brutal because I was that one kid no one talked to or wanted to hang around with.

The half-hour lunchtime felt excruciatingly long and painful. I know it was only 30 minutes, but jeez, did it feel like an eternity! Neither was going through the line and showing my free lunch card a walk in the park for me.

At that table, there were like 2 or 3 other kids that no one hung out with or even talked to. Ironically, even though we were the kids that no one talked to or wanted to hang out with, neither did we try to approach each other. Today, I find that to be very odd, and try to cope or understand why that was. Was it that somehow we had accepted our roles as nobodies within the school, not even good enough to approach one another or speak among ourselves, or was it an abysmal lack of confidence?

Sitting there, I observed the different groups of kids hanging out among each other, chit-chatting away happily with burst of laughter and big old smiles on their faces. It was a sight to behold and used to mesmerized me. I felt like a lone man lost in the middle of the desert coming upon a mirage. At the hierarchy of the groups were the kids known as JAPS, an acronym for Jewish American Prince.

They were easily recognizable, but different from the Hasidic Jews we were used to seeing in New York City. JAPS all wore a gold chain with the Star of David, and some of the boys donned a yarmulke, besides wearing designer jeans, polo shirts, Nike sneakers, and Nike nylon track suits, which were what the cool kids were wearing then, of course!

The school was located in a very affluent area with splendid homes, and one could easily tell by just looking at them that the residents had significant financial means. This group, among the wealthiest in the school, resided in the vicinity of the school, on Alton Road, or in homes right on the water with boats.

Their parents would occasionally pull up in luxury cars like Mercedes Benz, BMWs, Jaguars, and even SAABs. None of them ever drove American made cars or Toyotas! Back then, driving one of those afore-mentioned European vehicles was considered common knowledge that you were doing well economically.

There are also the White trash kids who, a lot of the time, wore cool but worn rock concert t-shirts.

They looked like they were not doing that great economically. Japs were Caucasian, but so were the White trash kids. I always wondered how people could be of the same stock, so to speak, yet be so different. Back then, I understood somewhat why I was poor. Also, being that I had heard about Overtown, I could see somewhat why many Blacks were economically at a disadvantage too.

Nevertheless, I found the disparity between the JAPs and the so-called White trash kids quite odd and an enigma.

Then there were the African American kids, who also tended to hang out together. It was easy to tell that they were of low income. I dare say that many of them did not even live on Miami Beach, where the school was located. There were no predominantly Black neighborhoods on Miami Beach, unlike in other areas of Miami. The Black kids spoke with a distinctive Black, Southern accent, unlike the Black Kids I knew in New York City. Their demeanor also differed significantly from the Black kids in New York City.

Ironically, many Black kids and White trash kids had one thing in common: a lot of them used to sell Dinosaur Eggs in school. Many transactions occurred, and these eggs changed hands between the students at Nautilus every day. They were quite popular.

I, on the other hand, liked candy bars. At Nautilus, I hoped that we would receive the fundraiser chocolate bars, like in New York City, that came in boxes that were convenient to carry because of the handles.

I always brought home at least two boxes filled with the World's Finest Almond chocolate bars ever! I never sold a single candy bar or box, even though they were to be sold for like 10 cents each! Instead, my siblings and I went through those chocolates as if they were a free gift for us to enjoy. Mom ended up paying for them later, though. However, Nautilus didn't have a chocolate-selling fundraiser like in NYC.

You also had the cool Latino Kids, mostly of Cuban ancestry, who seemed to be doing well economically. Due to my lack of information, I was surprised to see that some of those Cuban descendants were also Jewish.

One day, I observed one of the cool Cuban American boys. He had green eyes, light-colored hair, a tan complexion, and athletic build, he could had easily been a member of the musical group Menudo. He engaged in a lively and up-close conversation with a beautiful fair-skinned Cuban American girl who had dyed her hair blond.

He kept playfully kissing her on the lips every so often. Caught in the moment, he noticed me staring at them. Instead of feeling appalled, I was fascinated, wishing I could look like him and exude that level of confidence.

Suddenly, he locked eyes with me and boldly declared, 'She is my sister!' I just looked towards the floor and turned away. I couldn't comprehend why he felt the need to clarify their relationship, especially when it was obvious.

I wonder what went through his head when he caught me staring at them. Little did he know that I wasn't staring to condemn; on the contrary, I was highly impressed and yearning to possess his same level of confidence.

Last but not least, there were the groups of Marielitos, who exclusively spoke Spanish, were economically disadvantaged, and dressed similarly to me. The Marielitos formed a tight-knit community due to their shared background. They were often very loud, rowdy, and always appeared to be arguing or debating with each other, even when they were merely holding a conversation.

They were all in the ESOL class. On the first day of school, somehow, and/or based on mere appearance alone, I too had been enrolled in the ESOL class. I had no idea what that class was about either. While going to school in New York City, I had never heard of a class called ESOL!

Anyway, I showed up in that classroom, and after a while, the teacher asked me if I spoke English. I said yes, I do. She said I did not need to be there, so she got me out immediately.

Anyone might assume that, being a recent arrival like the Marielitos, and living in the same neighborhood on South Beach, I would naturally gravitate towards them and form connections. But I refrained from making friends with the Marielitos because, our experiences, desires, expectations and personalities were vastly different. In contrast, I thought in English, was deeply depressed, unhappy and always wishing to return to what I had considered to have been a better life while growing up in 1970s New York City. The school bus I rode on was called by the other kids at Nautilus the Banana Boat, which made me feel ashamed to ride on because most of the kids that rode it were Marielitos. Anyhow, the Marielitos used to give the bus driver a hard time because they were very loud and unruly. The driver had to now and then stop the bus to yell at them and ask them to settle down and keep it quiet. There was this one brown-skinned, curly-haired Cuban girl who was particularly loud, which the bus driver unabashedly christened her the Motor Mouth! The bus driver was a white guy that looked like the actor Perry King with a mustache and Ray-Bans on. It indeed was a clash of cultures and language barriers because, no matter how many times the driver yelled at them, it just seemed that the Marielitos did not understand why they should be quiet and had to settle down.

I remember one day, after school, our so-called banana boat was heading down Alton Road at a very good speed. There was a very big brown-skinned Cuban kid in the seat in front of me, who was standing while looking out the window. He was so elated; it was as if he had never traveled on a vehicle at that rate of speed and was like, 'WOO-HOO!' while he laughed happily.

He then looks at me and says, 'We Cubans love velocity!' I just nodded my head and thought to myself, 'Yeah, right, this is probably the first time you have ever traveled this fast.' What should I have responded? 'Oh, this ain't shit! When we visited my uncle in Canada and also flew to Ecuador, I'm pretty sure we were traveling at speeds that this bus could only dream about. And while we're at it, I've also been to Washington

D.C. and Niagara Falls too. By the way, celebrating the Fourth of July in 1976 for the Bicentennial was especially grand! Where have you been?'

But what could anyone expect from a kid who was always feeling sorry for himself, down and miserable? Anyhow, not that they would have believed me because, as far as anyone could see, I'm just another poor and disadvantaged kid who had never been anywhere.

Anyway, I would have never said it out loud and risk getting my butt kicked. Besides, that big Cuban kid was not a bad guy, and he always seemed jolly and always wore a smile on his face.

Similarly, this disconnection extended to other loner kids as well. Ironically, I didn't want to be a loner, my other wish was to fit in and be a part of the cool crowd. At P.S. 14 Queens, in the school cafeteria , I was always surrounded by the warmth of my classmates and friends, packed tightly, shoulder to shoulder.

However, at the Nautilus cafeteria, sitting at that mostly empty table, its expansive white top seemed to stretch out before me for miles and miles. It made me feel exposed and vulnerable, wishing to magically disappear, even though I was already practically invisible.

On my first day of school in 1981, I distinctly remember being the first to walk into my math classroom. It wasn't that I was rushing or making a deliberate effort to be there first; rather, unlike the other kids, I had no one to chit-chat and hang around the hallways with.

Unlike the many students that would take some time to socialize before heading to class or linger around their lockers and the halls in between classes.

Upon entering, I noticed a very thin young lady sitting at the desk. Assuming she was a fellow student, I inquired, 'Where is the teacher?' To my surprise, she responded, 'I am the teacher!' Her name was Ms.

Perez, a 28-year-old who looked much younger. Of Cuban descent, I was unsure if she was born in the States or if she and her family had migrated when she was very young after Castro took over Cuba. I developed a crush on Ms. Perez. She was not only very beautiful but also bore a striking resemblance to a Puerto Rican soap opera actress from the '70s named Johanna Rosaly, whom my mom used to watch on WNJU (channel 47) — only even prettier. Soon, I began making a nuisance of myself just to capture her attention. Whenever she had had enough, she would gaze at me with a stern look in her eye and say, 'ZEUS!' — pronounced in Spanish instead of English. It made me feel as if we shared some kind of bond or common understanding, being both Hispanic/Latinos. At times, I even sensed that she might have enjoyed it saying my name pronounced in Spanish somehow. In the evenings, I used to sleep with an old radio right beside my ear, without headphones. Whenever the song 'Just Once' by James Ingram came on, I would fall asleep fantasizing that Ms. Perez and I were in love. I still wonder where she is today. Like all things that brought me joy, whether tangible or just a dream, as usual, I have never forgotten her.

# 11

# HOPING FOR A MIRACLE

I started to skip school quite a lot. Regardless, I was never able to stay focused or concentrate on any schoolwork. All I did was daydream, reminisce, and wish for many things: the Atari 2600, a BMX bike, ONTV cable television, and GI-Joe action figures, even though they had shrunk drastically and were no longer as grand as the original GI Joes.

I believed the asking price around that time for an Atari 2600 was about $140, but being on welfare, that was well beyond our means. We lived on the first floor in a one-bedroom apartment on 529 15th Street in Miami Beach. The neighborhood was safe, nice, and sunny. Ironically, even though we had nothing except for three beds and a 19-inch color television, if we wanted to go to the beach, all we had to do was walk a couple of blocks and we were there.

One day, about a half a block away, on Drexel Avenue they were filming a scene of the Smokey and the Bandit movie, but without Burt Reynolds/The Bandit! There was a moment when they had stopped filming, and the late great Jackie Gleason sat in the squad car with the actor who played his son/junior in the passenger side. I am standing on the sidewalk 10 feet away from Mr. Gleason, who was sitting with the door open, with his body partially turned to one side and his left foot on the street.

I am staring at Mr. Gleason, and he is staring back at me. He looks straight at me, and now and then, he looks to one side and then back at me as if he was saying in his mind, 'What the hell is wrong with this kid?' or 'What the heck is this kid looking at?' But I believe it was just Mr. Gleason's natural body language, just like in the movies.

Little did he know that I was so happy, and maybe he kept wondering when was I going to wipe the smile off my face. Junior was right beside him and kept looking forward and back again at the crowd. He looked like he was still in character, or was that really his natural facial expression?

Next thing you know, an Asian guy who was part of the film crew—I do not know if he was the director or what—asked me and like three other kids to climb on the squad car and had us lay on our backs, side by side in a row, covering the rear glass. I have no idea why they asked us to cover the glass like that, maybe something to do with the sunlight, and neither did it dawn on me to ask.

Around that time, they had also filmed the movie called Porky's at the Feinberg Fisher school on 14th street, where my younger siblings, Johnny and Gina, went to. Anyway, I feel privileged to have made eye contact with Mr. Gleason, much better than when we saw Neil Sedaka at the Macy's Thanksgiving Day parade!

Nevertheless, the landlord had offered to pay my mother $50 per month to vacuum the stairs in that building. If memory serves me well, I believe there were four entrances to that apartment building. Additionally, she was tasked with polishing each of the embedded mailboxes on the side of a wall in each hall. Since the job was supposed to be done on Saturdays, my mother gave me the job, which I begrudgingly accepted.

I had become lazy and very self-conscious. I felt ashamed and embarrassed whenever a tenant saw me doing a half-ass job on the stairs. The thing is that I wasn't ashamed or embarrassed by doing such a lackluster of a job. I felt ashamed and embarrassed having them see me, a twelve-year-old boy, doing that type of work, even though it was only on Saturdays.

I don't know why I became lazy, severely lacking in motivation, self-conscious, and unfocused. Maybe it was because I had no friends, role model, or someone to advise and guide me. Mom was always busy with my baby sister.

One day, returning home from skipping school, it so happened that my mother, who must have been about 8 months pregnant, was across the street from me, walking down the same street I was on. She saw me first and called me. I turned to look, and there she was with her gloriously enlarged pregnant belly. Seeing her grossed me out and made me feel ashamed. I just wanted to jump out of my skin.

So I turned away and completely ignored her. I was not going to respond or walk over to her because I did not want to be seen with her. She just looked at me with astonishment I knew that I could not immediately continue on my way home.

I had no friends who I could go visit to burn some time, nor any money to go play some arcade game at the corner store and hang out for a couple of hours. So I had no choice but to just walk around Flamingo Park, then make my way back to Washington Avenue, and then down Lincoln Road before building enough courage and deciding to finally return home.

I walked around aimlessly, with a profound sense of dread that hung over my head like a dark cloud.

That day, I had already been out skipping school right after homeroom.  All I did was walk out the door that led to the teacher's parking lot.  Periodically grimacing and looking over my shoulder, and expecting someone to be there waving for me to return to school while I made my way towards Alton Road.

Once on Alton Road, it was a long stretch on foot towards South Beach. I used to take my time walking as slowly but as inconspicuous as possible. Nevertheless, always fearing being intercepted by Miami Beach police or Metro Dade, but that never happened.  Neither did I ever encounter anyone else walking down Alton Road, even though there were many houses along one side of Alton Road.

So, that encounter with mom added like 2 more hours to my day of skipping school because now I was skipping from returning home and had to walk around South Beach all over again. Anyhow, as soon as I returned home, my mother welcomed me with a belt and unleashed her fury upon me for making her feel indignant earlier that day. I do not know for certain, but maybe people feel that I was a very bad and mean little boy who did not love or respect his mother.

For that encounter, I caught a very bad beating.  If anyone would have come upon that scene, they would have seen a crazed pregnant woman beating a 12-year-old boy.

But even to this day, I remember exactly why I felt resentment towards my mother.  So I try to understand why I had turned into that child. I remember consistently taking into account our family's current situation.  Being that we were now living in Miami Beach after our perilous journey in Ecuador, financially, we were still at a disadvantage. Of course, our living conditions had improved by a lot, and thanks to the food stamp benefits, we had access to enough food, but we could not afford any luxuries, and neither were we able to have plenty of the stuff that we had been able to obtain while growing up in New York City.

My mother was not able to work because of her pregnancy, and neither was she able to look for any work after my baby sister was born. I also felt ashamed and somehow betrayed because I really felt that it was a very bad decision for my mother to allow herself to become pregnant by my father because, no matter what, he was never going to leave Monica and never did!

My father's relationship and consequent marriage with Monica lasted for 45 years until his death in September of 2020. By comparison, my father married my mother in 1965, but by 1975 my father was already involved in an extramarital affair with Monica.

So having no income with an extra mouth to feed used to worry me and make me feel insecure. I also felt ashamed and worried about what other people thought seeing a pregnant woman with 4 kids with no husband or income.

Regardless, being on welfare always made me feel ashamed, even as a young child, I inherently knew that for some reason it was not Kosher, so to speak. Even though I was a child, these things used to weigh heavily on my mind, and I excessively juggled all of those thoughts and worries every day.

But no one ever did ask me how I felt. In the eyes of my mother, I was just a shitty kid who deserved a beating!

Because I lacked so many things, like friends, a role model, stuff, and still was wishing to return to that past from NYC, or hoping to magically become one of the cool kids at Nautilus, I really hated living in Miami Beach. Part or all of the aforementioned was the reason for my great sense of unhappiness and lack of motivation. I just felt worthless.

I remember, late at night, after everyone had gone to sleep, I would sneak into my mother's purse and steal a few $1 food stamps. The next day, I would go to a corner store and buy a TWIX or Mars Bar for 25 cents. With great embarrassment, I would pay for the candy bar with a $1 food stamp. The shopkeeper would give me 75 cents change, which I would use to play PAC-Man or Donkey Kong at that very store. On other occasions, I would save those 75 cents each time until I had $2 worth of coins, then head over to a toy store on the corner of Lincoln Road and Washington Ave. and purchase a Star Wars or GI-Joe action figure for $1.99. Ironically, I hated the $2.99 BoBos Mom got for me from the local Pantry Pride, but I sure loved those action figures for $1.99.

Anyway, Mom never caught me, or maybe she decided not to say anything and just let me be, out of guilt.

The cleaning supplies were in a storage closet in the building. I found all of the cleaning supplies in a storage room. The landlord, or someone, had stored a few other things in there that caught my eye. There was a catcher's mitt, baseball glove, a 3-foot-tall outdoor plastic lighted Santa Claus, and last but not least, a blue Penny board which was exactly the same as one I had owned in New York! I shamelessly took all of those things with me back to our apartment.

Out of all those things, the Penny board was the jewel of the bunch, and I would definitely put it to good use. I couldn't wait to feel myself gliding down Collins and Ocean Drive, so that I could feel the cool wind in my hair or maybe try to learn some stunts while making a nuisance of myself on Lincoln Road. Even though I took the baseball gloves, I never played with them, so they just laid there, gathering dust.

I was supposed to polish the mailbox and vacuum the stairs every Saturday, but I only did the job every other Saturday and with lackluster effort because what I looked forward to doing on Saturdays was riding that Penny board. It gave me a great sense of freedom. I could go as fast as I wanted and as far as I wanted. Waiting an entire month to get paid $50 was also discouraging and seemed like an excruciatingly long time for me. Once again, it was what I felt and how I saw it. Maybe if I knew how to communicate without any fears of reprisals and/or being dismissed, I probably would have asked to be paid $12 after completing the job. But I no longer knew how to stand up for myself and just kept juggling all those thoughts in my head.

One day, in my homeroom class, I overheard some kid talking about his broken Atari. Now, for me, owning an Atari was high on my bucket list.

I imagined that this could be the opportunity of a lifetime to finally possess, even if broken, an Atari 2600! The desire to own an Atari was so great in me that I thought I could surely fix it regardless of any technical knowledge because my desire was so intense and divine!

Because of that desire, I was certain that the video game gods would grant me that wish. Once in my hands, without much fuss or tinkering, I was certain I could make that broken-down Atari work!

So, I offered the kid $40 for his broken Atari, and that kid was like, 'WOW, you are going to give me $40 for my broken Atari!' and I was like, 'YES, YES, YES!' Somehow, we were both very happy with that deal. He brought me the broken Atari the very next day, so no skipping school for me that day, no siree! The heavens had finally come together, and the planets had aligned in my favor!

The following day, I was standing by my locker, that kid, wearing his navy blue Nike nylon track suit, approached me looking all conspicuous as if some drug deal was about to go down. He opens his book bag, and I took a peep, and I swear I could hear the angels sing, 'Hallelujah, Hallelujah, Hale, lu, lu lu jah, yay!' Sure enough, there it was, the Atari 2600, in all its furniture brown color and black plastic glory!

I thought to myself, "Poor sucker, I'm sure it's just a loose wire," and handed that kid the two $20 bills. He grabbed the money and started to make a 180 even before he had completed saying thanks!

I could not wait to make it home so that I may fix it and finally be part of that home video game-playing crowd. I can see myself playing Pac-Man at home while listening to the Pac-Man Fever song!

> *'Cause I've got Pac-Man fever (Pac-Man fever)*
> *It's driving me crazy (driving me crazy)*
> *I've got Pac-Man fever (Pac-Man fever)*
> *I'm going out of my mind (going out of my mind)*
> *I've got Pac-Man fever (Pac-Man fever)*
> *I'm going out of my mind (going out of my mind)*

Well, after connecting the 2600 to our television and much tinkering and fussing, unplugging it and once again plugging it back in and hoping for a miracle to make the Atari work, it never did, as if destiny would have had it be any different. Even though paying $40 for a broken-down Atari somehow felt so righteous!

Ironically, as of this writing, the $40 that I paid for that broken-down Atari in 1981 is worth about $140 in today's money, which would have been the amount I needed back then to be able to buy a new Atari in 1981.

# 12

## DEBORAH SEGAL

Whenever I decided to stay a full day in school, walking down the halls at Nautilus Junior High between periods, there was this kid who was always surrounded by friends. He walked just like Iron man did after he shot a missile at the tank, turned around, and started walking away even before the tank exploded. All I knew was that he was indeed a JAP, and it was obvious that he was the most popular kid in school and very, very cool. He was built like a wrestler, with curly blond hair and blue eyes, reminding me of Chris Atkins from the movie "The Blue Lagoon."

Since I never talked to anyone, I had no idea what his name was. A few years later, our paths crossed in the most unusual and surprising of ways. Because of that encounter many years later, I finally knew his name, which is Dennis Salinas.

One of the many girls I sometimes saw around Dennis was a girl named Deborah Segal. The first time I saw her, I immediately developed a crush on her. In the hallways, I always kept an eye out for her. She was easy to spot because of her great hair, and her Jordache designer jeans fit her perfectly, unlike any other girl. So, I went out of my way to find out her name. Rather than approaching any other student and asking what her name was, I went to the school library and meticulously combed through the yearbook until I found her.

Sure enough, there she was, with a pretty smile gloriously garnished by a set of braces. With her blue eyes and blond hair cut in a Farah Fawcett kind of hairstyle. She was the most beautiful girl I had ever seen. She resembled a younger version of Farah Fawcett!

One day, I saw her at her locker with a couple of her friends standing beside her. I came up with the grand idea of writing her a secret admirer note. As I walked by, trying to look inconspicuous with my man-on-the-moon-slow-motion walk, I tried to count the lockers from top to bottom and side to side to pinpoint her exact locker location.

So, that night at home, while listening to I-95 FM, I waited for inspiration and hoped to hear songs like "Waiting for a Girl Like You," "Don't Stop Believin'," "Up Where We Belong," "Open Arms," and even "Centerfold" from the J. Geils Band – all enough to inspire me, etc.

Anyhow, since I considered us to be polar opposites, I decided to write something corny about the contrast that existed between her and me. It went something like this,

*'You have never seen me, but I have seen you. Your hair shines like the sun, and your blue eyes are like the sky.*

*But I am the night and a dark eclipse. As long as you know that I love you, it would be enough to brighten up my nights.*

***Signed Anonymous***

I felt bereft of so many things, that lying there at night reminiscing about the brief glimpses that I had caught of Debbie was enough to bring me joy.Whenever I heard the song "Waiting For A Girl Like You,"

I would imagine that was our song, even though I believed she did not know I existed. Nevertheless, as soon as I heard the synth sound at the beginning of that song, I can clearly see myself falling into another dark and endless abyss, as fantasies of her and I being in love bombarded my mind like fireworks bursting in a darkened sky, while simultaneously trying to grasp onto and prolonged those many glimpses of her throughout the halls of Nautilus Junior High as I fall and fall...

*So long, I've been looking too hard*
*I've been waiting too long*
*Sometimes I don't know what I will find*
*I only know it's a matter of time*
*When you love someone*
*When you love someone*
*It feels so right, so warm and true*
*I need to know if you feel it too*

The following day, I was ready to deposit my secret admirer letter through the slot of Debbie's locker. I walked slower than ever before, making sure that there weren't many students around.

As soon as I approached her locker, I was hit with tunnel vision! While I was trying to count the lockers to make sure I had pinpointed it correctly, everything started to move before me as if it were an earthquake. It was like trying to watch images on TV while someone was pulling and pushing the television side to side.

Regardless of all that craziness, I chose the locker. Still, my fingers felt as if they were tentacles with a mind and a will of their own as I continued to fumble while trying to drop my secret admirer note in that locker. Good grief, I had become such a coward!

I mean, in New York City, after we moved away from President Street, I no longer had Richie to stick up for me or to fight for us. So back then, in Queens, when involved in a confrontation, I was always ready to stand up for myself. I learned to take a stand from watching Richie. Since it was always Richie, Cano, Lionel, and me, we used to fight and wrestle among ourselves, all in the name of fun. Thus helping me pick up a thing or two when it came to fighting.

Two of my most memorable fights took place in Queens. I was in the third or fourth grade. My opponent was a classmate, I no longer remember the reason for the fight, nor do I remember his name, even though we became cool after the fight. He was a Black heavy set kid, spoke with a high pitch voice, and was easily a head taller than me. I actually used to look straight up when speaking to him.

Anyway, the fight was after school, in the middle of winter, there was still snow on the ground, so, like most kids we had on our padded parka coats with hoods that had that fury thing that I always hated because it made my face itch. We exited the school on the side of Van Doren Street.

Anyhow, since my opponent was much larger than me, I decided to attack first and fast. So, as soon as he was in front of me, with both my hands, I grabbed him by the front of his Parka and pulled with all my strength to spin and throw him, hopefully to the ground.

Instead, his back crashed with the school's metal gate. He just stood there, closed his eyes, and began whimpering like a toddler. I was deeply surprised; I really had anticipated a monumental fight, but instead, I ended up feeling like a bully.

Which was something that I had never been. Richie always stood for being brave no matter how big of a challenge you were faced with. I had witnessed Richie fight kids that were bigger than him and never backed down. Anyway, I just walked away feeling terrible and never have forgotten that.

Afterwards, we actually became cool with each other. Now and again, he would invite me over to his home to play with a very cool home pinball machine. Every time I visited, his elderly grandfather was there reading a newspaper in their living room. Their apartment seemed dark and desolate, and devoid of many things.

His bedroom looked empty and free of clutter; it was just his bed and that cool pinball machine, and it did not look like he had many toys, like we did. There was a certain warmth and vibrancy missing.

Unlike our apartment, which was always bright, noisy, and with many activities going on, like Mom cooking and yelling at us to complete our homework while we ran in and out of the yard simultaneously watching our favorite cartoons.

I got the impression that he was being raised alone by his grandfather. I never bothered asking him if he had a mom and dad. Even then, I recognized that it could be something too delicate and private to be asking about, and neither did I wish to bring up any sad memories by asking, just in case it turns out that his parents were deceased or had abandoned him somehow. Anyway, back then, If I had known that he was probably an only child living alone with his grandfather, I would have never fought him.

The other fight I had that I remember very well was with another kid from school, a white kid. Once again, I do not remember why we even fought. I do remember coming down Otis Ave alongside my cousin Alex. That white kid and his older brother were across the street from us as we walked by. They were in front of 105-34 Otis Ave, which is where they lived. For some reason, we started cussing at each other. As soon as my cousin Alex sensed there was going to be a fight, he ran away quick fast! I was too proud and was not about to back down, so I crossed the street ready to rumble!

So there I was, kicking and punching and rolling all over the snow with both of the brothers. The snow had been shoveled and piled high against the light pole. Every time I would cut loose from my two opponents, I would scramble up the pile of snow and jump in the air trying to land on either one of them. I had always enjoyed playing King of the Mountain, where anyone who reached the top of the 6-foot-tall pile of snow could claim to be the king of the mountain and challenge anyone to knock them down to be the new king. But this was the real deal and a real-life Royal Rumble.

After those two other kids could not keep up with my relentlessness or was it pure recklessness, so they quit and started to walk away, now and then looking over their shoulder with a look of concern on their faces as if they were saying, 'That mother effer is crazy!' I, on the other hand, was like, 'Come back and fight, chickens!' They never came back out, so I stood down and started walking home. My mother was shocked and asked, 'What happened?' I just stood there looking gloriously beaten up, but proudly exhibiting my scratches, lumps, and bruises as if they were medals of honor!

Anyway, after finally depositing that dumb anonymous note, anyone else would have felt relief and elated, but not me. All I did was prove to myself that I was severely lacking in many ways. I mean, how hard of a challenge could it be to drop a note through a locker's slot!

Regardless, as soon as the bell rang, I headed towards Debbie's locker. I stopped and started rummaging through a folder, acting as if I was looking for some notes or something. She was not there yet, but there was some other dark-colored haired girl there first in the vicinity of Debbie's locker.

Once again, I am falling into the dark abyss as I see that dark-colored haired girl reading my note! Through my shock and all of the fumbling, I had chosen the wrong freakin' locker and missed my shot!

It was over, another chapter in my long book of failures had closed in on me again. I did not even bother to try again, accepted my fate, and continued to marinate in my depression, lost and drowning in the sauce.

However, on the days I did not skip school, I would still be on the lookout and try to catch a glimpse of Debbie, so that I could go home, put on I-95 FM, and wait for those romantic songs to come back on, playing the memory of the glimpses of Debbie over and over again.

Due to all the skipping school and disruptive behavior, I particularly targeted my social studies class, doing my best to annoy Mrs. Sawyer, my teacher there. She was an elderly Black woman who, from the looks of it, should have been retired because she used to fall asleep on us in the classroom. I would blurt out, 'Paranoia, Mrs. Sawyer!'

I had gotten that from the Kinks' song 'Destroyer'. Whenever she addressed me, unlike Ms. Perez, she would call me by my last name Pluas, but would pronounce it Ploo-Ass! As a result, I found myself frequently serving week-long stints at Nautilus Junior High's C.S.I. class. While C.S.I. stood for Classroom for Special Instruction, I had proudly christened it as Classroom for Stupid Idiots.

The supposed C.S.I. instructor was named Mr. Walker. He looked like a young version of Morgan Freeman. By the way, I use the term 'supposed' because we rarely received any substantial instruction. In terms of academic work, I recall him distributing just a single sheet at a time, each containing a handful of non-challenging math problems. And trust me, they were a walk in the park and very easy, even for me! Mr. Walker was essentially just babysitting us.

The student desks at C.S.I. were arranged along the walls of a very small classroom, more akin to the size of an office. There are two doors to the C.S.I. class. When you enter through Nautilus' main entrance, there's a door to the left that leads to Mr. Walker's office. If you continue and take a left turn down that wing, you'll find another door on the left, which is the entrance to the C.S.I. classroom.

So, there are two available doors to enter the C.S.I. class. You can also access Mr. Walker's office by going through an archway from the C.S.I. classroom, and vice versa.

Mr. Walker had his desk on the right-side wall of his office. Whenever we got too loud and rowdy in the C.S.I. classroom, Mr. Walker would lean back in his chair.

Without having to get up, he could look through the archway and ask us to keep it down, or else! I genuinely enjoyed my stints in C.S.I and wished I could be there for the entire school year. I even considered giving up skipping school altogether if I could stay in C.S.I. permanently. Perhaps it was because there were never more than like 8 students at a time. Additionally, we got to go to lunch first, having the whole cafeteria to ourselves. The kids in C.S.I. were friendly, non-judgmental, and kept it real. Or was it just a display of common comradeship being that we were but a few stuck in the same boat, so to speak. I guess I felt at home with the rest of the misfits.

There was this light-skinned Black girl who served as Mr. Walker's student aide. A few years later, every time I saw Jasmine Guy on TV, she always reminded me of Mr. Walker's student aide. Anyway, she was cute, and you could tell she had a crush on Mr. Walker.

One day, some white kid, that looked like Tommy Shaw from Styx, and who was from the white trash group of kids, was scratching down his pants. A black girl was like, 'Ooh, you nasty!' and the kid says, 'I can't help it, I got jock itch!

I had no idea what jock itch was and thought it was another scary disease like AIDS! I remember clearly when that whole AIDS scare thing was being propagated on the nightly news. According to popular belief, AIDS had like started and was out of control in Florida because of the Haitian refugees who were being blamed for bringing AIDS over to our shores—something to do with monkeys too.

My mother once told me, 'Don't ever go taking a leak in an alley somewhere because if an infected person with AIDS had also taken a leak in that same alley, my stream of piss could cause the AIDS-infected piss on the ground to splash on me, and so too will I get AIDS.' She told my sister Mildred that if she ever had to use a toilet while not at home, she should not sit on the toilet completely, but instead, she should have her butt hovering over the toilet while going.

Somewhat alarmed, I asked that kid how he got jock itch. He responds by saying that he got it after he had been in the pool. Immediately, I thought to myself, 'Oh no, can I possibly have jock itch too? I mean, I do go to the Flamingo Park Pool every now and then. So, with my luck, I more than likely have caught jock itch too!' The kid must have seen the look of concern on my face, so he explained, 'I got jock itch because I put on my pants while my swimming trunks were still wet!'

After that explanation, I felt like such a moron. I mean, how did I ever reach this level of obtuseness! I mean, while attending P.S. 14 Queens in the 3rd grade, I had independently detected a pattern in the dreaded 9 times table. While looking at the 9 times table, I noticed a pattern that made it almost as easy as the 5 times table. For example, whatever number 9 was going to be multiplied by, I would find the difference between that number and 10. Let's take 9 times 4 as an example. The difference between 4 and 10 is 6. Additionally, I would look at the number that comes before the one 9 is going to be multiplied by. In this case, it would be 3 before 4. Therefore, 9 times 4 is 36 because 3 precedes 4, and 6 is the difference between 4 and 10.

Anyhow, one day, during the C.S.I. class, I occupied the desk situated against the wall, right beside the C.S.I. classroom door. Everyone entering through that door would pass right beside me as I sat there.

All of a sudden, swishhh, and there was a breeze! As the door opened, I turned to look, and there she was walking past right beside me. I felt immediately afloat on a cloud as my eyes focused on those perfectly fitted Jordache jeans—or were they Sergio Valente's?

I don't know; all I know is that they were perfect. With each of her steps, she beckoned me to fall into a trance. The smooth motion of her hips, rising and falling, was a delicate balancing act between my heart and my soul...

She was the object of my desire, the one girl who I so much had wished to love. She had come by to drop off some paperwork for Mr Walker. So, there she had been, and just like the song says:

> *My eyes adored you*
> *Though I never laid a hand on you*
> *My eyes adored you*
> *Like a million miles away from me*
> *You couldn't see how I adored you*
> *So close, so close and yet so far*

As soon as she finished, she turned and started back towards where I was, and all I could do was to sit up and stare. Feeling numb all over, I am sure I must have had a dumbfounded look on my face. As the distance between her and I shortened, my eyes clung to her every move, wishing to attach themselves to her for all of eternity. I followed her every motion as she leaned forward and reached for the door.

As soon as she grabbed hold of the door, she turned towards me.

Since she was leaning forward and I was sitting ramrod straight, our faces were practically on the same level. She was an angel that had come down from the heavens to uplift a lowly soul. She turned towards me, looked me straight in the face, and gave me the sweetest smile with the most vibrant look in her blue eyes.

I was a deer caught in the headlights, and I immediately began to stutter a la Ralph Kramden, 'Homina... Homina... Homina!'

But wait, what have I done to deserve her smile? Does this mean she knew I existed? What should I do, what can I do? Who am I, what am I? This can't be right! Had she caught me trying to steal and catch glimpses of her in the hallways of Nautilus Junior High, or had someone caught me staring at her and went and told her, 'Hey, that loser is always staring at you!' Or maybe she had heard of my classroom antics just so I could be sent to C.S.I.

Or was it because she thought I was some kind of Billy Badass sitting there. Spotting glimpses of Debbie, whether up close or from afar, or receiving such a sweet and beautiful smile from her, made no difference. What if she had screamed as soon as she saw some dork approach her, or if other students had commented throughout the school about some dork trying to talk to the prettiest girl. Even though her smile seemed genuine, I just could not muster the courage to say anything to her. If I had known back then what I know today, I exactly know what I would have told her at Nautilus. I would have caught up to her and said,

*'Hi, Debbie, right? Although we don't know each other, I just wanted to say thank you. Things haven't been great for me lately, but your smile really brightened up my day. Thanks.'*

But I only excelled at getting myself put in detention, C.S.I., and skipping school. I was depressed, awkward and could never focus because I was always distracted and submerged in a quagmire of internal thoughts, feelings, and moods.

Perhaps becoming withdrawn was my way of coping with a time in my life when I didn't feel I counted for much in the external world. I just could not fit in or get on track , and considered myself already a great failure.  Soon after we would move away to the South West of Miami. Nevertheless, I never forgot Debbie Segal.

My lack of confidence, and shortcomings, perpetually condemned me to wonder what if. What if I would had drawn enough courage from within to finally say something to her but I was such and empty vessel, and so the song continues...

*(Like a million miles away from me) (You couldn't see how I adored you)*
*Oh the feeling, sad regrets (So close)*
*I know I won't ever forget you, my childhood friend*
*(So close and yet so far)*
*My eyes adored you*
*Though I never laid a hand on you*
*My eyes adored you*

# 13

## THE SCHWINN

Christmas 1982 came along, but we were never again able to celebrate Christmas as we had in New York City. The very last Christmas that my siblings and I enjoyed as children was Christmas of 1978 on Granger Street. Trying to catch some kind of Christmas spirit, I brought out that lighted plastic Santa Claus that was typically displayed outdoors.

Of course, I wasn't going to set it up outside, as someone, like the landlord, might accuse me of stealing it. So instead, I placed it in our mostly empty living room. It was quite pathetic and only made the environment seem more depressed.

My mother had placed a tall plastic plant thing in the corner of our living room. One of my younger siblings commented, 'Mom, is that our Christmas tree?' My mother found it hilarious and burst out laughing as if it were the funniest thing ever. However, I, on the other hand, did not find it funny at all because it felt as if Mom was laughing at us. I sure missed our old Christmas tree.

We arrived in Miami from Ecuador in the summer of 1981. In less than two years, Ecuador became a distant and surreal memory, and New York seemed like a lifetime ago. As far as becoming estranged from my father's family, as mom had planned it, had worked out to perfection.

Despite everything, I still longed for my grandparents, and deep down, I hoped that we could one day experience Christmas like the ones where Grandma clapped, sang, and encouraged us to dance to our favorite "Mi Burrito Sabanero" Christmas song.

So, seeking solace and attempting to recapture some of that Christmas spirit, I turned on the lighted Santa Claus in the cold, empty living room. It turned out to be another disappointment because all that Santa Claus was—a mere lamp emitting a depressing yellow light, devoid of any colors like those colorful Christmas lights.

If I could, I would kick it away and erase it from existence today.

We were never again able to enjoy another Christmas with those who had been closest to us and had been there to show us what Christmas was about during the very early years of our lives. Having been dragged into the middle of it all had been so unfair.

Once again, neither my siblings nor I received anything for Christmas. I should have gotten used to it by then, since the last time we received any gifts for Christmas was in 1978. Even though I had turned 13 years old earlier that year, I still wanted to have a lot of cool things.

The apartment building we lived in on 529, 15th street had a front door but also a rear door in the kitchen that led to an alley through the back of the building. In that same building, we had a neighbor who lived a couple of doors from us. She was a Cuban single mom with an 11-year-old son. I remember she used to wear a dark navy blue skirt suit to go to work. I have no idea where she worked, though.

For Christmas, she had gotten her son a very cool 20-inch Schwinn bicycle. I watched her son happily riding his brand-new bicycle, up and down the street, on Christmas day. The bicycle frame was a vibrant, shiny red, and its rims and handlebars were a shiny gold color. It had a competition number plate on the front of the handlebars and a pad set too. Around that time, it was the type of BMX bike that most kids had and rode. Saying that I yearned to be him would be an understatement.

After Christmas vacation was over, one day, returning home from having been out all day skipping school, I decided to enter through the rear door of our apartment instead of the front door. As I was coming down that back alleyway towards our rear door, lo and behold, there she was—shimmering bright and glistening under that splendid South Florida sun! I felt like a man lost at sea who had finally seen the light!

I only had a few feet to go, forcing me to think fast and decide what to do—or maybe not think at all and just behave with impunity. It was madness, trying to juggle conflicting thoughts while simultaneously figuring out how to act next.

No need for tunnel vision this time around. While my brain scrambled and short-circuited, my eyes honed in on the target. I was a bird of prey, swooping in on its unsuspecting victim. The linear perspective created by the building's wall to my right and the alleyway's wall to the left only served to help keep my eyes focused on the prize.

But wait! Was this just someone being careless, or was it a gift from the gods? I couldn't help but wonder. Why would anyone leave a beautiful Schwinn BMX bike unattended and alone in a back alleyway, at the most opportunistic moment, so that imprudence and impunity may come together in an unholy alliance along the path of one who desires many things, especially a BMX bike!

Or were the gods finally exercising some unconditional love my way, or is this just how the Butterfly Effect works? My many, many days of skipping school had turned into a well-structured routine. Despite all that meticulous planning, when I stumbled upon that Schwinn, as defenseless as it was beautiful, my carefully crafted structure went out the window, and I acted impulsively.

Regardless, the gods had maybe spoken and set up the scene for me to exercise my free will, whether right or wrong! So, I didn't bother to jump on the Schwinn and ride away with it. Besides, my rear door was only 20 feet away, and if I had decided to ride away with it, I feared that I would once again fumble and crash it into the wall. Instead, I just grabbed it by the handles and ran away with it.

I made it to my rear door and inside my apartment in no time at all! Having the Schwinn in my possession really felt like a gift and a prize, or a dream come true, considering it was something I had deeply desired but was seemingly unattainable due to our economic disadvantage. In a way, I kind of knew what the Boston Red Sox must have felt like when they won the World Series in 2004.


I knew Mom was going to have an issue as soon as she noticed the Schwinn, so I went into her linen closet and grabbed a white bed sheet to cover the Schwinn with. Being that I was, for sure, a neglected child, my need for self-gratification had fogged my mind so much that I really thought I could just cover a bicycle with a white bed sheet and believe that Mom would not notice it. Who was I kidding!

Well, Mom did notice, and with a look of concern, asked me where I got the bicycle from. The absolute and only answer I could come up with was that I had found it and expected her to believe that it had been as easy as that. Regardless of the look of concern upon her face, surprisingly, she did not press the issue. But how could she? Between her and my father, they had ruined my childhood and had made sure that I wasn't happy since the summer of 1979, be it directly and/or indirectly.

Anyhow, and besides my mother not having pressed the issue, neither did I hear any screams or an 11-year-old boy crying about his bike being stolen. Neither did anyone come along knocking on the door asking if we had seen a shiny red and gleaming BMX Schwinn bike. But how could they? This was a case of perfect timing, divinely executed for all the wrong reasons.

Nevertheless, I was emboldened, and even though the kid whose bike I had stolen was a neighbor and whose door was about 20 feet away from our door, I still could not wait to ride the Schwinn. So, I, at least, was careful enough to only ride it at night. I used to inconspicuously walk the bike towards the opposite corner, making sure never to ride the bike in front of our building or on 15th street.

Always grimacing, but never looking over my shoulder. As soon as I hit the corner, I would make a left on Drexel Avenue, jump on the bike, and haul ass out of there!

While coasting on a long stretch, I would look down at the front wheel as it spun and also gaze at the ground passing beneath me as I coasted over it. It felt magical, as if I were Aladdin riding high on a magic carpet, looking down at the earth in awe. It gave me a momentary sense of gratitude, relief and freedom. Relief and freedom from feeling sorry for myself all the time and from all those inwardly oppressive negative and depressing thoughts that crippled me, preventing me from functioning outwardly like a normal kid.

The Schwinn and I became one because it was as fast, as powerful, and went as far as I wanted it to go...


It was a splendid Saturday morning, bright and shiny. Some friends of my mother's friend were there to help us move. We didn't have much, so all they brought was a Ford F-something pickup truck. Anxiously, I kept wondering if people were watching us move out. One of the guys helping was about to grab the Schwinn. I intercepted him, saying I would take care of the bike. I stared down at the Schwinn, doubtful of what lay ahead. Would it become an object of turmoil after bringing me so much joy? Overwhelmed with fear, doubts, and possibly regrets, I wondered if Karma was about to expose me and pass me the bill. I grabbed the Schwinn by the handlebars, just as I did when I stole it. This time, with no rush, I slowly walked the bike toward the front door, feeling the walls closing in on me. Reaching the archway, I could hear my heart beating against my chest. I took one last deep breath as I scanned the horizon. It felt as If I were about to walk onto a minefield. Would I continue to be the invisible kid, or would the spotlight be on me as I walked through the archway with the stolen, but beloved Schwinn?

Nevertheless, that will be a story for another day.

# 14

# EPILOGUE

My father neglected and disregarded our well-being for the love of an adolescent woman. He was never there when we needed him the most. I knew I could never count on him for much of anything, and we never fully reconciled. In his presence, there was always that awkward silence present. For him, the well-being and love of a beautiful young woman were prioritized over the well-being of his wife and, worse, his very own children.

He left us behind without hauling us along with him; we were something to be forgotten and not remembered. Whenever he was in Ecuador, he never called. When he returned to New York City, it was to work for a few weeks, purchase more merchandise, and then return to his beloved Monica. My mother, too, disregarded her own children's well-being when she uprooted us and subjected us to what we endured for a marriage that, according to my father's actions, was already over.

I question whether either of my parents truly understood what genuine love meant. Why did my mother prioritize something else over her own children's well-being? Was it due to a misguided sense of love? I don't know how our lives would have unfolded if we had stayed in New York City, but the odds there would have been more in our favor. At least we wouldn't have been exposed to the poverty, trauma and drama that we experienced in Ecuador.

Was my mother acting on a whim, driven by her ego, or fueled by a desire to outdo the other woman? To forcibly piece together that which was irreparable, regardless of who got hurt or destroyed in the process?

To be fair, during our time in Ecuador, my father would spend some nights with Mom. Perhaps he was still feeding her lies, giving her the impression that the marriage wasn't over and that there was still hope, despite his serious relationship with Monica.

That might explain why, when we arrived in Miami, Mom was already pregnant with my baby sister, Diana. Mom named her youngest daughter after Lady Diana, whose wedding was televised just a month before my baby sister was born.

Interestingly, Monica was never able to get pregnant; however, a couple of decades later, my father and Monica adopted a child. Regardless, by Mom becoming pregnant while my father was dating Monica could have been her way of showing Monica that her lover was still involved in the creation of children with his actual wife—a kind of symbolic statement or a metaphorical slap in the face!

# 15

# AFTERWORD

Reflecting deeply on the genuine reasons and motives behind professing love is crucial. Without a true understanding when those reasons, expectations, or beliefs crumble, it sets the stage for profound pain and chaos. As a witness to my parent's actions and the impact on my siblings and me, I've come to realize the lasting effects of misaligned love, both during childhood and throughout adulthood.

They both did it because of love. My mother made regrettable decisions because she still loved my father. Simultaneously, my father's unfortunate choices were driven by his love for another woman.

So we, their children, were collateral damage in a war about love that my parents waged against each other.

What I learned from that experience is that caring and a good conscience is what needs to be nurtured.

Because without them, individuals may, at times, neglect the well-being of their supposed loved ones and compromise their moral principles in the name of 'love'.